KAZAKHSTAN

By
Catherine Bradley

The Millbrook Press
Brookfield, Connecticut

©Aladdin Books Ltd 1992

Designed and produced by
Aladdin Books Ltd
28 Percy Street
London W1P 9FF

First published in the
United States in 1992 by
The Millbrook Press
2 Old New Milford Road
Brookfield, Connecticut 06804

The consultant is Dr. John Channon of the School of
Slavonic and Eastern European Studies, London.

Series Design: David West
Designer: Rob Hillier
Editor: Jen Green
Picture Research: Emma Krikler

Library of Congress Cataloging-in-Publication Data

Bradley, Catherine.
    Kazakhstan/by Catherine Bradley
  John Channon, consultant.
        p. cm -- (Former Soviet States)
      Includes bibliographical references and index.
      Summary: Discusses the ethnic mixture, political
situation, and economy of the former Soviet republic of Kazakhstan.
      ISBN 1-56294-308-1 (lib. bdg.)
      1. Kazakhstan--Juvenile literature. (1.Kazakhstan.)
  I. Title. II. Series.
  DK903.B73 1992
  958'.45--dc20   92-2243 CIP AC

Printed in Belgium

CONTENTS

INTRODUCTION   4

THE STATE TODAY   6

PEOPLE AND PLACES   8

NOMADS AND HORDES   10

UNDER RUSSIAN RULE   12

THE ADVENT OF COMMUNISM   14

WORLD WAR II   16

KUNAEV'S KHANATE   18

THE IMPACT OF PERESTROIKA   20

THE CITIZENS OF KAZAKHSTAN   22

STANDING ALONE   24

OUTLOOK   26

FACTS AND FIGURES   28

CHRONOLOGY AND FAMOUS PEOPLE   30

INDEX   32

INTRODUCTION

Kazakhstan lies at the center of the landmass of Eurasia. Since the fifteenth century its fate has been bound up with that of Russia, first as part of the Russian Empire until 1917, and then, after the October Revolution, as a member of the communist Soviet Union. But in the 1980s Soviet leaders admitted that communism was not working. In 1991 the Soviet Union was dissolved, and Kazakhstan became a member of the newly formed Commonwealth of Independent States (C.I.S.).

Kazakhstan is the second largest state to emerge from the breakup of the former Soviet Union, being second in size only to Russia itself. It has a wealth of natural resources, including many minerals, such as lead, copper, coal, and oil. It also produces sheep, grain, vegetables, and other agricultural produce. But like other countries of the former Soviet Union, Kazakhstan faces many changes as it adjusts to its new-found independence.

4

Arctic Ocean

Zemlya Frantsa Josifa

70° E

80° E

90° E

Severnaya
Zemlya

Kara Sea

100° E

110° E

120° E

130° E

140° E

150° E

160° E

170° E

Novo Sibirskiye
Ostrova

Laptev Sea

Kolyma

Bering Sea

Lena

Yenisey

Sea of Okhotsk

50° N

Sakhalin

RUSSIAN FEDERATION

JAPAN

Trans-Siberian Railroad

Lake Baikal

40° N

Vladivostok

MONGOLIA

NORTH KOREA

SOUTH KOREA

CHINA

| 0 | 250 | 500 | 750 | 1000 | 1250 MILES |

| 0 | 500 | 1000 | 1500 | 2000 KILOMETERS |

THE STATE TODAY

Kazakhstan's iron and steel industry is mainly concentrated in the north.

For all its vast territory and wealth of resources, Kazakhstan faces an uncertain future as an independent country. Part of the reason for this lies in the history of its relationship with Russia. For almost three centuries, the Kazakh people have suffered as a result of Russian domination.

Apartments built with Soviet subsidies

Kazakhstan has long been a land of opportunity for the Russian and Soviet Empire. During the nineteenth century large numbers of peasants from Russia, Belarus, and the Ukraine flocked to the unpopulated plains of Kazakhstan. In the twentieth century this tradition continued, as the Soviet Empire deported unwanted peoples from European Russia and elsewhere to Kazakhstan. Economically Kazakhstan provided raw materials for Soviet industry and food for the Soviet peoples.

However, the Soviet Union did not just exploit its neighbor; there were some advantages in the relationship for Kazakhstan. From the 1950s it received massive subsidies from the Soviet state – almost 20 percent of its revenue. This was used to build up Kazazkhstan's cities and industry.

The Kazakh people themselves represented only one-third of the population of Kazakhstan, being outnumbered by Slavs (Russians and Ukrainians). However, Kazakhs had favored status in their country. They were allowed to dominate the local government, and claimed preference in administrative jobs and university places as their due. In many ways Soviet Russia regarded Kazakhstan, with its large Russian and Slavic population, as its closest ally.

With the breakup of the Soviet Union, the Kazakhstan leader, Nursultan Nazarbayev, was anxious to protect the special relationship with Russia. In December 1991, however, he bowed to the inevitable and joined Russia, the Ukraine, and Belarus in founding the new Commonwealth of Independent States.

Industry

Today, Kazakhstan is still very dependent on Russia economically. It has a trade deficit with the other countries of the former Soviet Union. In 1988 this deficit amounted to eight billion rubles (about $4.4 billion.) Kazakhstan's industry is mainly concentrated in the north, near the border with Russia. The industry there has been built up in the last 40 years and is an extension of the southern Siberian industrial region. Planned by economic experts in Moscow, it supplies raw materials at low prices to Russia, and has to buy chemicals and other products for its factories at high prices.

The planners in Moscow insisted on building up heavy industry, that is, chemicals, steel, and other products. These industries produce a great deal of pollution. Toxic chemicals in the atmosphere have led to many health problems, including an increase in infant mortality. Kazakhstan's industrial labor force is mainly made up of Russians, Ukrainians, and other non-Kazakhs. This is a factor which has tended to cause resentment among the Kazakh people themselves (see page 9).

Agriculture

Almost half of Kazakhstan's population is employed in agriculture. Kazakhs traditionally kept vast herds of animals. In central and southern parts of Kazakhstan, natural pastures still provide good feeding grounds for sheep, cattle, and goats. Kazakhstan is also an important grain-producing area. The land is organized into large state farms and collectives. In 1988 Kazakhstan produced 22.6 million tons of grain. However, there is a constant problem with erosion, as winds blow soil from the flat steppes, or grasslands.

Harvesting grain on the vast Kazakh plain

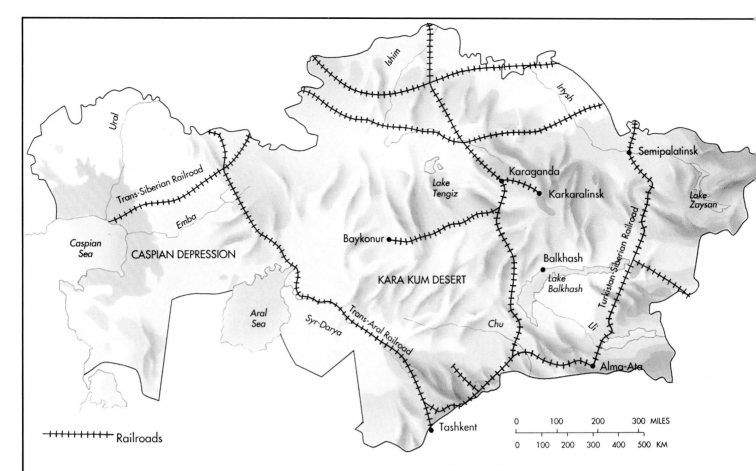

PEOPLE AND PLACES

Kazakhstan covers a vast territory, stretching from the Caspian Sea in the west to the Tien Shan and Altai mountains in the east, a distance of about 1,200 miles (1,900 kilometers). To the north and west lies the Russian Federation, to the east China, and to the south Turkmenistan, Uzbekistan, and Kyrgyzstan. Kazakhstan contains lands of great variety, from the deserts of Kara Kum, through grassland steppes, to lush orchards near the capital Alma-Ata. The climate is harsh, with very hot summers and very cold winters. There is little rainfall over much of the country, and water is a scarce resource.

Because of the lack of rain, the state farms in the south must irrigate their land to grow cotton and to produce hay and fodder for the winter feeding of animals. However, the increasing demand for water in Kazakhstan and in the other central Asian countries has led to ecological problems. The large inland seas, the Caspian and Aral, contain much less water than they used to. This has had a devastating effect on the fish and plant life. Salt levels in the soil have increased, and some areas have become deserts. Attempts to irrigate the land have not been well managed; overwatering of the soil has led to widespread damage and loss of crops. Plans to divert waters from Siberian rivers to Kazakhstan and central Asia were abandoned in 1986. Throughout the country the overuse of pesticides has created pollution problems.

Other issues

Kazakhstan was one of the former Soviet republics which had nuclear missile bases stationed on its territory. The Soviet army tested its nuclear weapons in the Semipalatinsk area and its chemical and biological weapons in other sites. The contamination from these tests will take years to clean up.

Under the communist system women were entitled to equal rights and were well represented in the local governing bodies, known as soviets. Since the breakup of the Soviet Union this is being reversed. Kazakhstan may not be willing to pay for women's rights to education and child care in the future.

Harvesters receive a loaf baked from new grain.

The people

The Kazakhs are a Muslim, Turkic-speaking people. They represent around 40 percent of the population, and are the leading people of Kazakhstan. Russians have been moving to the area since the eighteenth century, and now form about 38 percent of the population; Ukrainians constitute another 5.5 percent. Muslim settlers arrived in the late nineteenth century. Uighurs and Dungans from China also settled in the southern parts of Kazakhstan. Many nationalities were deported to Kazakhstan during World War II, including Germans, Crimean Tatars, and Meskhetians. There are also Uzbeks and Kyrgyz living in the south.

Although Kazakhs dominate the education system – 70 to 90 percent of students are Kazakhs – they do not have the technical skills to work in industry. Such jobs have traditionally gone to Slavs. The very high birthrate among Kazakhs in the 1980s has led to increasing unemployment among young Kazakhs, which in turn has led to resentment of the non-Kazakhs, who have the jobs.

In the last 25 years there has been growing nationalist sentiment among the Kazakh people. In 1979 there were riots in Tselinograd over rumors that land would be set aside to give the local Germans their own self-governing region. Anti-Russian feelings also grew as Russians became more dominant in the Soviet Union's leadership in the late 1980s. In June 1989 there were riots in Novy Uzen, the center of the gasoline industry, when Kazakhs attacked Caucasians. The Caucasians, who were technicians in the gasoline industry, fled, creating a shortage of skilled workers.

NOMADS AND HORDES

For centuries nomadic peoples have lived on the steppes of Kazakhstan. Herding families lived in tents made of animal skins, and moved from pasture to pasture with their animals – mainly sheep and goats, but also horses, asses, and camels, which were used for pulling carts. The lack of water on the steppes meant the nomadic families had to keep moving. Herds provided the families with food (mainly milk, not meat) and materials such as wool and leather. The nomads produced goods and animals which they could trade for grain, vegetables, and fruit at markets, usually in the cities of the more settled peoples of the south (around Bukhara and Samarkand). Horsemen dominated the steppes from Mongolia to Hungary for 2,000 years. War became their way of life because without it, the leaders could not provide the horsemen with the goods they needed.

Kazakh horses approach the Tien Shan Mountains.

The Kazakh horse
Breeding over hundreds of years has produced this rugged animal. The Kazakh horse is small, with a coat of different colors. It weighs about 700-800 pounds (320-360 kilograms). Over the centuries the horse was important to the peoples of Kazakhstan, and its military uses became obvious. Kazakh horses could outrun all other animals. The nomads discovered that raiding markets on horseback often produced more wealth than haggling.

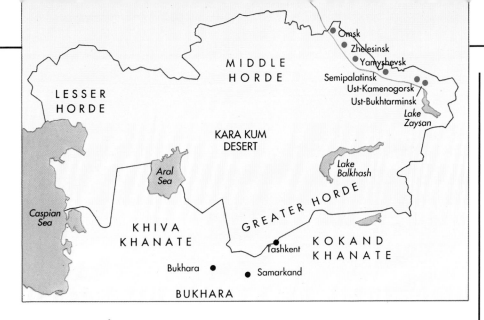

Map labels:
MIDDLE HORDE
LESSER HORDE
Omsk
Zhelesinsk
Yamyshevsk
Semipalatinsk
Ust-Kamenogorsk
Ust-Bukhtarminsk
Lake Zaysan
KARA KUM DESERT
Aral Sea
Lake Balkhash
GREATER HORDE
Caspian Sea
KHIVA KHANATE
Tashkent
KOKAND KHANATE
Bukhara
Samarkand
BUKHARA

- ● Russian forts
- ● Towns
- —— Present boundary

KAZAKHSTAN C 1600-1750

0 100 200 300 MILES
0   250   500 KM

In the sixth century the Kazakh nomads formed part of the Turkish Empire – a loose grouping of nomadic peoples. During the eighth century they came under pressure from the Mongolians farther east.

The Golden Horde

In the tenth century the Mongolian Khitans were the dominant tribe in the area. They were followed by the Karakitai, who were themselves ousted by a group of formidable Mongols led by Genghis Khan. These Mongols, known as the Golden Horde, swept all opposition aside as they spread westward, and in 1240 the Russian city of Kiev fell to them. Meanwhile an offshoot of the main Mongol army,

known as the White Horde and led by Orda, Genghis Khan's grandson, dominated the area of Kazakhstan.

These Mongol armies, however, were beset by internal problems as rivals challenged the leaders, and other groups of nomadic peoples developed their own fighting skills. If the armies on horseback were badly led, they could lose ground and booty. By the end of the fourteenth century the Mongol Empire was falling apart. Two new powers emerged, the Nogais (another offshoot of the Mongols) and the Uzbeks.

The term Kazakh began to be used around 1520, when the people of Kazakhstan were known as the Uzbek Kazakhs. At

this time, two leaders from the White Horde moved to neighboring Mongolistan and began to build up a Kazakh dominion, or "khanate." By the early sixteenth century Kazakhs were united under Kassim Khan, who ruled 1511-18, and had 200,000 horsemen. Under Kassim Khan the Kazakhs controlled the steppe region. His three sons succeeded him, but by the seventeenth century the khan's power weakened. The Kazakhs split into three hordes. The Greater, Middle, and Lesser Hordes spread between the Tien Shan Mountains and the Ural River.

A Mongol leader

Squatting on the earth floor of his tent, a Kazakh herdsman crushes rice between two stones.

UNDER RUSSIAN RULE

During the seventeenth century the Kazakh hordes faced attacks from the powerful Oyrats in the east. They fought together temporarily under Tauke Khan (1680-1718) and in the 1720s succeeded in defeating the Oyrats. This success was short-lived, however; the alliance soon fell apart as new power struggles started up.

Meanwhile the Russians were beginning to advance through the Kazakh steppe. The Romanov dynasty, which ruled Russia from the sixteenth century, was pursuing a policy of expanding Russian territory to the east, south, and west. In 1718 the Russians established a fort at Semipalatinsk, and a year later one at Ust-Kamenogorsk (see page 11). The Kazakhs thought the Russians might protect them against the eastern invaders, and accepted the Russian tsar's protection. At the time the Russians called the Kazakhs the Kirgiz, to distinguish them from the Cossacks' – the remnants of the Mongol armies in Crimea and on the Volga.

Russian influence
At first the Russians left the Kazakhs to rule themselves. But in the 1820s, the Russians abolished the power of the khans. This resulted in Kazakh uprisings, but by the mid-nineteenth century Russia was firmly in control. The Kazakh lands were divided into four provinces, and Russian and Ukrainian peasants were encouraged to settle there and farm the steppes.

The Russian rulers also encouraged Tatars to move in and convert the Kazakhs to Islam. Although the Kazakh khans had followed Islam, their people continued to follow the older religions. The tsars may have thought Islam would make the tribes easier to control.

Part of the empire

The Kazakh nobles received Russian education and became influenced by nationalist ideas. Kazakh culture became more developed and many writers became prominent. The first Kazakh newspaper appeared in 1910. But there was a deep and growing resentment against the Slavic settlers who were taking away Kazakh lands.

World War I

Russia entered the war in 1914, siding with Britain, France, and the United States against Germany and Austria. In 1916 the Russian tsar, Nicholas II, tried to mobilize the Kazakhs to fight. The Kazakhs objected, killing many Russian settlers before they were massacred by the Russian army.

Tents were made of skins stretched over a framework of sticks.

Communism

During the nineteenth century Karl Marx developed a theory about how society was organized which became known as Marxism; as applied later in the Soviet Union it was called communism. Marxism was a theory about industrialized countries. Marx argued that wealthy people used their capital (money) to make more capital by investing it in industry. He thought that people who worked and provided their labor were being exploited, and that workers should overthrow capitalists in a revolution. They should gain control of land and industry and build a fairer society. His ideas were developed by the revolutionary Vladimir Lenin (below).

THE ADVENT OF COMMUNISM

Revolution in Russia

In 1917 the Russian war effort collapsed. Soldiers started to leave the army in large numbers. This led to much uncertainty, and there were strikes by workers in many Russian cities. In March, Tsar Nicholas II abdicated, and a government of politicians was formed. Lenin saw his opportunity to seize power; in October he led the Bolshevik Revolution.

The Bolsheviks (who became known as communists after 1918) were opposed by many groups, but this opposition never became

Bolshevik troops storm the tsar's Winter Palace in 1917.

united. After three years of fighting, Lenin and his supporters had established control of most of the Russian Empire. The empire became known as the Union of Soviet Socialist Republics (U.S.S.R.) or the Soviet Union.

Civil War

In 1917 the tsarist government in Kazakhstan collapsed, and the nationalists, known as the Alash Orda, formed a Kazakh government. During the Civil War the Alash Orda backed the communists,

Crop failure, combined with the upheaval of Civil War, led to starvation in many village communities.

Joseph Stalin (1879-1953) was born in Georgia, and trained to be a priest. He joined the revolutionary Bolshevik Party and took part in the Russian revolutions of 1917. In 1924 he became leader of the Soviet Communist Party. Stalin got rid of his opponents in the party by purges. He imposed a modernization program for industry and agriculture which was forced through using terror tactics. Any opponents to communism were sent to labor camps, and millions died. Stalin led the Soviet Union to victory over Nazi Germany in World War II.

who they thought would grant them their independence. By 1919 the communists had gained control of Kazakhstan, and in 1920 the Kirgiz (that is, Kazakh) Autonomous Republic was set up. But the Civil War had disrupted farming, and a famine followed. Some 1.5 million people are thought to have died, though many Kazakhs with their flocks escaped to China and Afghanistan.

In 1926 the name of the republic was changed to Kazakhstan, and the communist rulers of the newly founded Soviet Union started to interfere in Kazakh affairs. The former Alash Orda leaders were killed.

Collectivization

Stalin became leader of the Soviet Union in 1924. Stalin wanted to change the Soviet Union from an agricultural country into an industrial power. This involved taking land from the peasants and organizing it into large state farms and collectives.

The collectivization program was launched in 1929. In Kazakhstan the nomadic herders had to give up their flocks and settle down; the flocks were to be tended by teams of herders, not by families. The Kazakhs resisted this strongly. Many farmers and peasants killed their animals rather than hand them over. Eighty percent of the Kazakh flocks were destroyed. This led to food shortages and starvation in the 1930s.

In 1935, the fifteenth anniversary of the republic, collective farms were given deeds to their lands.

Kazakh women deputies vote at a meeting of the Supreme Soviet in Alma-Ata in 1939.

WORLD WAR II

In 1936 Kazakhstan officially became part of the Soviet Union as a union republic. Its population had been decimated by the political upheavals of the previous 20 years. In 1897 there had been 3,800,000 Kazakhs. By 1926 the number had only grown to 3,986,000, and by 1934 the number of Kazakhs had fallen to 2,900,000.

Outbreak of war
In 1941 the Soviet Union was invaded by Germany, under the command of Adolf Hitler. Having occupied Poland, France, Belgium, and Holland, Hitler coveted the wheat fields of southern Russia and the Ukraine, and the oil fields of the Caucasus.

The invasion was resisted by the Soviet Army. The conflict had a great impact on Kazakhstan because of Stalin's decision to use the country as a dumping ground for certain "problem" nationalities during the war.

Deportations – The Soviet Germans
During the war Stalin adopted a very harsh policy toward several nationalities (see the map on page 23). He thought the Soviet Germans, living mainly on the Volga, might help the invading Nazi Germans, even though most Soviet Germans had come to Russia in the late eighteenth century. In 1941 some 800,000 Germans were deported from European Russia to Siberia and Kazakhstan. They were given only basic shelter, and little food. Soviet Germans were also deported from the Soviet Union by the Nazis, who reached the Volga region in 1942.

The Crimean Tatars
Another group that was forcibly deported during World War II was the Crimean Tatars. Descended from the Mongols, the Tatars had settled in Crimea and by 1926 formed a quarter of the local population. They

suffered particularly during the collectivization and purges, and when Germany invaded in 1941, Stalin feared the Tatars would help the enemy. However, the area was overrun by the Germans in 1942, before any deportations could take place.

By 1943 the German advance had been halted, and the Soviet Army began to reclaim the land that had been lost to the invaders. When the Soviet Army recaptured Crimea in 1944, the Crimean Tatars were severely punished. In May 1944 some 220,000 Tatars were evacuated at gunpoint and sent to Uzbekistan and Kazakhstan. Many died on the way and the Tatars claim that 110,000 had died by 1946. They endured particularly bad conditions. Their villages in the Crimea were razed and all traces of their culture removed.

In 1941 the Soviet Army launched a counterattack against Germany. Above: Red Army troops head for the front.

The Meskhetians

The Meskhetians came from around the Turkish border in Georgia. They were never in danger of being overrun by Germans during World War II, but they suffered a fate similar to that of the Crimean Tatars. In November 1944 many were deported, along with other Turkic groups, to central Asia and Kazakhstan. It is thought that 200,000 were deported and 50,000 are thought to have died from hunger and cold.

Peace

In 1945 World War II ended in victory for the Allies – the United States, Britain, France, and the Soviet Union. But victory did not bring an end to the hardships endured by the peoples whom Stalin had deported to Kazakhstan. Many people were not allowed to return to their homes. Those people who were permitted to return, such as the Soviet Germans who had been deported by the Nazis, were treated especially harshly on their return to the Soviet Union.

Stalin died in 1953. After his death many deported nationalities were allowed to return home and were rehabilitated. But some were not permitted to return, including the Crimean Tatars and Meskhetians.

KUNAEV'S KHANATE

After Stalin's death there was considerable unrest in Kazakhstan. In 1954 Leonid Brezhnev was sent by the Soviet leader, Nikita Khrushchev, to sort out problems there. Brezhnev formed close links with a Kazakh, Dinmukhamed Kunaev, who was to succeed him as first secretary of the Kazakh Communist Party in 1956.

Plowing up the Virgin Lands

In 1954 Khrushchev launched a policy of plowing up the "Virgin Lands" to increase agricultural output in the Soviet Union. Thousands of Russian and Ukrainian farmers were sent to plow up the steppes – 62 million acres (25 million hectares). Khrushchev criticized Kunaev for the economic difficulties of his republic and Kunaev resigned. In 1964 Khrushchev himself was ousted and Brezhnev became general secretary of the Soviet Communist Party. At the same time Kunaev returned to power in the Kazakh Communist Party, and dominated political affairs in the republic until 1986.

Brezhnev's man

As one of Brezhnev's protégés, Kunaev was able to secure Soviet resources to develop Kazakhstan. Northern Kazakhstan became an industrial center and the cities were developed. Alma-Ata expanded greatly, and many

Leonid Ilyich Brezhnev (1906-82) was a land surveyor who joined the Communist Party in 1931. He fought in the army during World War II. Under Khrushchev, he was sent to Kazakhstan to supervise local matters. He succeeded Nikita Khrushchev as leader of the Communist Party, but shared power with two others. He allowed local leaders, such as Kunaev, to run things their own way and the Soviet economy stagnated. After his death, his daughter and other family members were found to have traded on the black market in gold and in diamonds.

Slav settlers erect tents in the Virgin Lands in the 1950s.

Dinmukhamed Akhmedovich Kunaev (born 1911 or 1912) was a mining engineer who joined the Kazakh Communist Party in 1939. He rose through the party and became friendly with Leonid Brezhnev. In 1956 he became first secretary of the Kazakh Communist

Party, but resigned after criticism from Khrushchev. He resumed office again in 1964. Kunaev became a Politburo member under Brezhnev. He ruled Kazakhstan with his family and gained money from imaginary agricultural projects to build Alma-Ata. He fell from power in 1986.

monumental government buildings were constructed, some even decorated with gold leaf. Kunaev also became a member of the Politburo – the small group of communist leaders who were in control of the Soviet Union.

It was a time of seemingly great prosperity. Many people enjoyed a higher standard of living, but in fact the republic of Kazakhstan was slipping behind Moldova, Armenia, Azerbaijan, and Georgia in terms of economic development. Kunaev ran the republic as a family enterprise. He and the other members of his family enjoyed enormous privileges and great wealth.

Corruption

Kunaev undoubtedly used his position to promote his family's welfare. His brother, Asqar Kunaev, was president of the Kazakh Academy of Science. Other family members held jobs in the provinces for which they were overpaid. The minister of Higher and Secondary Education was fired for taking bribes. The group around Kunaev had control of 247 hotels, 414 guest apartments, 84 cottages, 22 hunting lodges, 350 hospital beds, and other facilities such as private aircraft, which were used for personal rather than for official purposes.

Leonid Brezhnev died in 1982. Yuri Andropov succeeded him as Soviet

leader and launched a drive against corruption.

Purging the party

From 1982 Andropov sent teams of anti-corruption agents to tour the republics and purge the Communist Party of corrupt elements. In 1984 they were busy in neighboring Uzbekistan. Kunaev knew they would soon be in Kazakhstan and he helped to expose a corrupt Russian minister there.

But in 1984 Yuri Andropov died. He was succeeded as Soviet leader by Konstantin Chernenko, who promised to continue Andropov's drive against corruption. However, Chernenko died the following year.

THE IMPACT OF PERESTROIKA

In 1985 the Soviet Communist Party elected a young and vigorous leader, Mikhail Gorbachev, as its new general secretary. Gorbachev immediately set about reforming the Soviet system through the new policy of *perestroika,* or restructuring. He also introduced a policy of *glasnost,* or openness, which allowed people to express their views more openly, and criticize communism. Gorbachev also tried to speed up the drive against corruption.

Kunaev's replacement

In December 1986 it was announced that Kunaev was being replaced by a Russian, Gennadii Kolbin. There was an immediate response – young Kazakh people protested over the appointment of a Russian. Official accounts stated that there were 3,000 demonstrators, and in the ensuing riots two people died and 200 were injured. This was the first political mass demonstration in Soviet history since 1927!

Kazakh protest

Essentially the demonstration was an expression of anti-Russian feeling by Kazakh students. Kolbin remained in charge and tried to placate the Kazakhs by creating committees on interethnic problems. A special commission discovered that there was

Mikhail Gorbachev was born in 1931 and joined the Communist Party in 1952. In 1985 he was made general secretary of the party and tried to steer the Soviet Union on a reform program. He never quite succeeded in forcing through the necessary economic reforms. In 1991 opponents tried to force him from power. They were foiled, but Gorbachev's importance declined as a result. In 1992 he stepped down as the Soviet Union dissolved into independent states.

Antinuclear protest

much antipathy over language; Kazakhs felt that their language was regarded as second-class, since the administration only dealt with requests presented in Russian, and Russians hardly bothered to learn Kazakh. Eventually in 1989 Kazakh was made the official language of the republic. In June 1989 Kolbin was replaced by Nursultan Nazarbayev, a reforming Kazakh.

Meanwhile the reforms of the Soviet economy were leading to many problems in Kazakhstan. There were food shortages and a severe lack of housing, because the building programs

Nursultan Nazarbayev became the first elected president of Kazakhstan in 1990.

could not keep pace with the increase in population. There were pollution problems too; both industry and agriculture had damaged the environment and this was creating health problems.

In 1989 a Semipalatinsk Oblast Peace Committee announced that there had been radiation leaks in the area as a result of nuclear weapons testing. In September 1990 an explosion at the Ulba nuclear fuel processing plant at Ust-Kamenogorsk led to beryllium gas being released into the atmosphere. A week later 60,000 people demanded the closure of the plant and Nazarbayev pressed for compensation.

Nazarbayev began to reform the communist economy of Kazakhstan. His government set in motion various moves to control trade, economic activity, and land. He launched a privatization program that would put land and industry in private hands – after nearly 70 years of state ownership.

The collapse of communism

In August 1991 the news broke that the Soviet Army and anti-Gorbachev leaders had tried to seize power in Moscow. As a result, the Communist Party was discredited and the move away from communism was speeded up. The Kazakh Communist Party changed its name, but in fact most of its people remained in power.

In late 1991 Nazarbayev's position as the Kazakh leader was confirmed when he was reelected president of the republic. He joined the Russian, Ukrainian, and Belarussian leaders in forming the Common-wealth of Independent States. After centuries of rule from Moscow, Kazakhstan became an independent state.

THE CITIZENS OF KAZAKHSTAN

The presence of non-Kazakh nationalities in Kazakhstan has been a source of conflict in the country historically, and may well prove an important factor in the newly independent state.

The Slavic peoples

By far the most important groups of immigrants in Kazakhstan are the Russians and other Slavic peoples. After the emancipation of the serfs in 1861, when peasants gained their "freedom" and were allowed to leave their masters' lands, many impoverished people sought their fortune in central Asia. By 1897 some 400,000 Russians had settled in Kazakhstan.

The greatest wave of Slavic immigration occurred in the first half of the twentieth century. By 1916 there were over a million non-Muslim people in Kazakhstan. These included Jews, Belarussians, Mordvins, Germans, Poles, Tatars, and Bulgarians.

Crimean Tatars demand the right to return to their native land.

Another wave of Slavic immigration to Kazakhstan occurred in the 1950s, when Russians and Ukrainians were again encouraged to move there to develop the Virgin Lands and industry. Throughout the 1960s and 1970s Russian technicians moved to Kazakhstan.

In the 1980s anti-Russian feeling led to more and more Slavic people leaving Kazakhstan and going to the Baltic states, which promised a higher standard of living. This may no longer be an option, but many Russians may want to live in the Russian Federation. President Nazarbayev is anxious that these skilled workers should stay, or industry and agriculture might collapse. The Ukrainians and Belarussians face the same pressures.

The Germans

There are nearly one million Germans living in

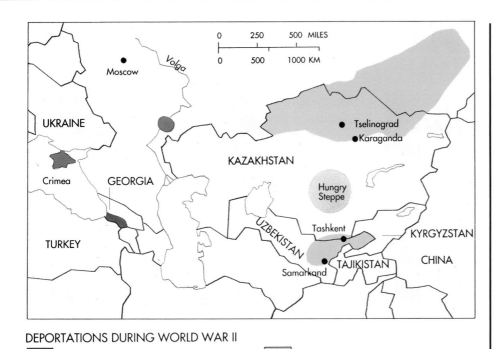

DEPORTATIONS DURING WORLD WAR II

- ■ Meskhetians
- ■ Soviet Germans
- ■ Crimean Tatars

- ■ Deported Meskhetians
- ■ Deported Germans
- ■ Deported Tatars

Kazakhstan. They work mainly in agriculture and live in the north. The Soviet Germans suffered particularly from Stalin's policy of deportation during World War II (see pages 16-17).

After the war was over, the Soviet Germans continued to live in very poor conditions until pressure from the West German government led to some improvement. In 1964 the Germans were rehabilitated, but they were not allowed to return to their former home around the Volga. In 1979 rumors that land would be given to the Germans to form their own self-governing region led to riots in Tselinograd. Today many Germans and their descendants are trying to leave Kazakhstan.

The Crimean Tatars

There are over 330,000 Crimean Tatars in Kazakhstan. They were also forcibly deported during World War II. Even after Stalin's death they were not allowed to return home, unlike many other deported nationalities. In 1956 the Tatars launched a campaign to return to their lands. Eventually in 1967 a decree was published which stated that the Crimean Tatars had been unjustly treated. The campaign to return continues, despite the persecution of its leaders.

The Meskhetians

Like the Crimean Tatars, the Meskhetians were not allowed to return home after Stalin's death; they had to campaign for their return. They would like to go back to their homes on the Turkish border near Georgia, but the Georgians are not eager to accept them. There are about 150,000 Meskhetians who have nowhere to go.

Soviet Germans await departure to Germany in 1989.

STANDING ALONE

The shrinking of the Aral Sea has devastated the wildlife of the region.

Kazakhstan is the leading nation among the former republics of the Soviet Union in central Asia. It is the most industrialized and the most Russified, containing the largest Slavic groups. Although the central Asian republics face similar economic problems, they are all looking for outside partnerships as a way of developing their economies.

Ecological problems

Kazakhstan and its neighbors share a common shortage of water. From 1960 to 1975 the level of the Caspian Sea dropped by 8 feet (2.5 meters), as its waters were diverted elsewhere for agricultural use. It has since risen again

but 2,700 square miles (7,000 square kilometers) have dried up. The Aral Sea has lost 23 feet (7 meters) and has shrunk by 5,000 square miles (13,000 square kilometers). Its shores have moved 62 miles (100 kilometers). This has led to loss of plant and animal life and to soil problems, as the dried-up areas are very salty. Kazakhstan and its neighbors need to cooperate in order to solve the problem of the drying of the Aral Sea, but in the rush to improve economic conditions in the area, this may not happen.

Islamic fundamentalism

Kazakhstan and its central Asian neighbors fear the spread of Islamic fundamentalism. In Iran the setting up of an Islamic state, where mullahs (priests) have political power, has led to economic problems and difficult relations with the United States and Europe. The republics want to prevent the same thing from happening within their own borders. The Islamic Renaissance Party is therefore banned in most of these countries.

Security

It is quite likely that Kazakhstan has some 2,000 nuclear warheads on its territory. Russia, the Ukraine, Belarus, and Kazakhstan – the four states with nuclear weapons – have agreed that the weapons can be used only with the consent of all four countries. President

Nazarbayev stated in 1992 that there were no more tactical weapons on Kazakh territory and that weapons would be destroyed in Russia, according to the agreements between the former Soviet Union and the United States. However, there have been persistent rumors that a few nuclear warheads in Kazakhstan have been sold to Iran.

The Russian soldiers on Kazakh soil are restless. In February 1992, 500 soldiers at the Baikonur space station mutinied because of their poor living conditions. President Nazarbayev was one of the few Commonwealth leaders eager to make the Soviet Army into a Commonwealth Army. However, he has now agreed that Kazakhstan will have to organize its own army, something which the country can ill afford.

Historically the border between Kazakhstan and Kyrgyzstan is disputed, but this is not an urgent matter. For both these central Asian countries, finding partners in economic development is a more important and pressing concern.

Kazakhstan must find markets for iron and steel.

The space station of Baikonur was built by the Soviet Union – but who will use it in the future?

OUTLOOK

What does the future hold for Kazakhstan? Will the country be able to resolve its internal and external problems? For the moment President Nazarbayev is treading a careful path. He knows that Kazakhstan cannot achieve economic independence swiftly, and that Kazakh industry desperately needs its skilled non-Kazakh workforce to remain. For the time being, Kazakhstan must continue to produce raw materials for processing factories in other parts of the former Soviet Union, chiefly Russia, because there are no other markets open to it yet.

President Nazarbayev has launched a program to privatize industry. This is being done by selling to the highest bidder in an auction, by offering enterprises for sale by tender, and by selling shares in state enterprises.

Privatization

The first task of Nazarbayev's government was to pass the laws necessary to establish Kazakhstan's ownership of state-controlled enterprises. It has also passed laws allowing foreign investment, setting up free economic zones, and granting licenses for various kinds of economic activity, such as mining, drug manufacture, and lumber production.

New markets

President Nazarbayev would like Kazakhstan to join the European Community, but he is also looking eastward. He has appointed a Korean-American economist to advise him. The border with China has been opened, and Chinese businessmen have been looking at business opportunities. There may also be trading opportunities to the south, with Pakistan.

Democracy

President Nazarbayev rules Kazakhstan in an authoritarian way. He has not allowed the Alash opposition group to register as a political party. The Alash group wants the Russians to leave Kazakhstan. Leading members of Alash are in jail, awaiting trial for disturbances in Alma-Ata in December 1991. Nazarbayev has been elected by the people as president. But he is not allowing the people much say in how the

The younger generation faces many changes.

President Nazarbayev consults with Russia's president, Boris Yeltsin.

Many factories are in need of modernization.

country is run, unlike the situation in neighboring Kyrgyzstan, where President Askar Akayev is striving to make his country "the real center of democracy in central Asia."

For all its mineral and other resources, Kazakhstan faces an uncertain future as an independent state. The country needs to develop trading relations with its neighbors and further afield. It needs to reform its agriculture and industry so that it can produce goods, such as wool and leather, which will bring money into the country. Then gradually people's living conditions will begin to improve. Adjusting to free trade and market economics will take many years, as all the states of the former Soviet Union are finding.

FACTS AND FIGURES

Area: 1,049,000 sq miles (2,717,300 sq km)
Capital: Alma-Ata
Population: 16,793,100 (1991 estimate)

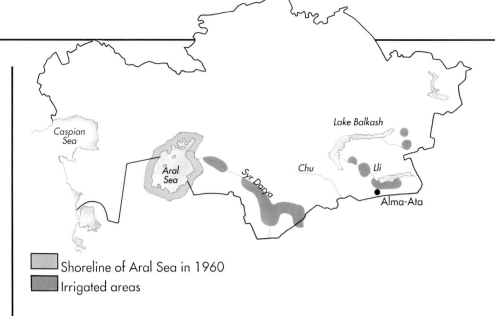

Shoreline of Aral Sea in 1960

Irrigated areas

Water

There are over 7,000 streams and rivers in Kazakhstan. Most of them drain into the Caspian and Aral seas or into lakes. The most important rivers are the Irtysh, the Ural, and the Syr-Darya. Many rivers are small and dry up in the summer. Kazakhstan contains 48,000 lakes, the largest of which is Lake Balkhash (6,830 sq miles / 17,700 sq km). Both the Aral Sea and the Caspian Sea face ecological disaster as they dry up.

Agriculture

Three-quarters of farmland is used for crops, the remainder for orchards and vineyards. In 1988 Kazakhstan was responsible for 15.5 percent of the Soviet Union's agricultural output. Kazakhstan is a major meat-producing area. Sheep are bred for their wool and astrakhan pelts. Cattle, goats, pigs, and poultry are also raised. In the south, fruits and vegetables such as melons, sugar beets, tobacco, rice, hemp, cotton, and grapes are produced.

Natural resources

There are more than 90 different minerals found in Kazakhstan. It has major deposits of coal, iron ore, lead, zinc, copper, and oil. The Tengiz oil field is one of the world's largest. In May 1992 Kazakhstan and the U.S. corporation Chevron signed an agreement to develop the Tengiz oil field – the biggest partnership to date between a U.S. corporation and a former Soviet republic. Kazakhstan also has nickel, tin, cadmium, bauxite, gold, silver, tungsten, and cobalt.

Industry

Kazakhstan is a major supplier of raw materials to the Russian Federation. It has large chemical plants in Karaganda, Aktyubinsk, Balkhash, and other cities. Kazakhstan produced 25 million tons of oil in 1990. Fuel and

Grain output by republics

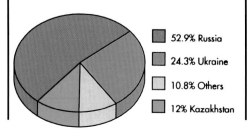

- 52.9% Russia
- 24.3% Ukraine
- 10.8% Others
- 12% Kazakhstan

Oil output by republics

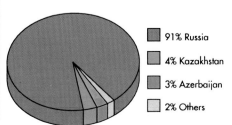

- 91% Russia
- 4% Kazakhstan
- 3% Azerbaijan
- 2% Others

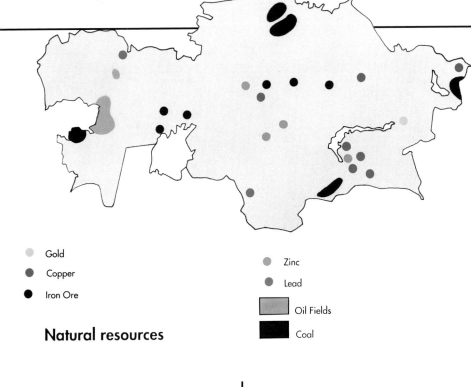

Natural resources

- Gold
- Copper
- Iron Ore
- Zinc
- Lead
- Oil Fields
- Coal

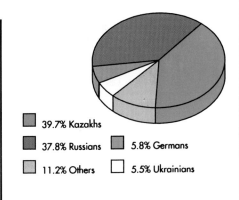

- 39.7% Kazakhs
- 37.8% Russians
- 11.2% Others
- 5.8% Germans
- 5.5% Ukrainians

19671

power are supplied by the Karaganda and Ekibastuz coal basin and by hydroelectric plants on the Irtysh River. Factories produce cast iron, steel, rolled metal, cement, machines, mineral fertilizer, textiles, footwear, and other goods. A significant space center was established at Baikonur, 150 miles (240 kilometers) northeast of the Aral Sea, in the desert of central Kazakhstan. Most of the workers there are Russian.

Steel output by republics

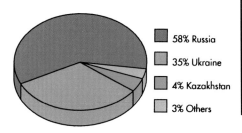

- 58% Russia
- 35% Ukraine
- 4% Kazakhstan
- 3% Others

Transportation

Kazakhstan is crossed by the Trans-Siberian Railroad, which was built at the end of the nineteenth century and links Russia's west and east. Running west to south there is the Orenburg-Tashkent line, and from south to north in eastern Kazakhstan there is the Turkestan-Siberian line, which was completed in 1930.

Cities

The capital city, Alma-Ata (meaning father of apples), was known as Verny until 1921. Alma-Ata and its suburbs have a population of 1,130,000. Kazakhstan has 82 towns and 197 urban settlements. These include the older towns, such as Semipalatinsk

(317,000 inhabitants), Petropavlovsk, and Uralsk as well as the newer, planned cities such as Karaganda (the mining center with 617,000 inhabitants), Ust-Kamen-ogorsk, and Rudny.

Language

The Kazakh language is a central Turkic language. It has borrowed many words from Russian, Arabic, Persian, and Mongol, as well as Chinese, Tatar, and Uzbek. Kazakh schools also teach in Russian, Uzbek, Uighur, Dungan, and Tajik.

Religion

The Kazakhs are Muslims. Their conversion dates from the work of Tatar mullahs (priests) in the nineteenth century. Their beliefs are said not to be very strong. However, there is a revival of religious beliefs among young Kazakhs.

Ethnic mix

CHRONOLOGY AND FAMOUS PEOPLE

A.D. 425-577 Huns dominate central Asia
1137-1216 Kara Kitai Empire in central Asia
c1160-1220 Genghis Khan (exact dates unknown)
1219-21 Mongol conquest of central Asia
1237-41 Mongol conquest of Russia
c1450 Formation of the Uzbek Khanate
c1500 Formation of the Kazakh Khanate
c1600 Formation of the three Kazakh Hordes
1731 Lesser Kazakh Horde comes under Russian rule
1740 Middle Kazakh Horde comes under Russian rule
1846 Greater Kazakh Horde comes under Russian rule
1854 Founding of Verny (Alma-Ata)
1891-1903 The Trans-Siberian Railroad is built
1906 Trans-Aral Railroad is completed
1914-18 World War I
1916 Uprising in Kazakhstan and central Asia
1917 Two Russian revolutions
1918-20 Civil War;

Genghis Khan (c1160-1227) was a Mongol ruler and military genius who founded the largest land empire in history. His harsh training methods transformed tribespeople into a well-disciplined army. With this army he conquered Mongolia, central Asia, and northeastern China.

formation of an independent state in Kazakhstan
1920 Kirghiz (that is, Kazakh) Autonomous Soviet Republic formed
1922 Creation of the Union of Soviet Socialist Republics; Stalin becomes general secretary of the Communist Party
1929-37 Collectivization and purges
1930 Turkestan-Siberian

Alexander II (1818-81) became tsar of Russia in 1855. He was known as the "tsar-reformer." In 1861 he passed a law freeing serfs from ties to their masters. This led to large numbers of Russian and Ukrainian peasants moving to central Asia. He was assassinated by terrorists in 1881.

Railroad is finished
1936 New Soviet constitution; Kazakhstan becomes a Soviet Socialist Republic
1941 German invasion of the Soviet Union; mass deportation of Soviet Germans, Crimean Tatars, Meskhetians, and other nationalities to central Asia begins
1945 World War II ends
1953 Stalin dies

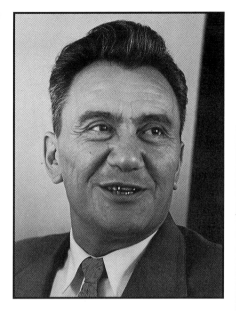

Nikita Sergeyevich Khrushchev (1894-1971) was the son of a Ukrainian miner. He rose to become leader of the Communist Party after Stalin's death, and launched the "Virgin Lands" program to plow up the steppes. In 1964, after his plans' failure, he was removed from office.

Dinmukhamed Akhmedovich Kunaev (c1911-) rose through the Communist Party through his friendship with Brezhnev. He became first secretary of the Kazakh Communist Party in 1956, and again in 1964. He used his office to advance his family until he fell from power.

Nursultan Abishevich Nazarbayev (1940-) served on the Kazakh Communist Party Central Committee with Kunaev, but led the opposition to Kunaev in 1986. In 1989 he became first secretary of the Kazakh Communist Party, and in 1990 became the first elected president of Kazakhstan.

1953 Khrushchev becomes Soviet leader
1959 Virgin Lands project leads to plowing up of the steppes in Kazakhstan
1964 Khrushchev is ousted; Brezhnev becomes one of the new Soviet leaders; Dinmukhamed Kunaev is appointed leader of the Kazakh Communist Party; Soviet Germans are rehabilitated

1982 Brezhnev dies
1985 Mikhail Gorbachev becomes general secretary of the Communist Party
1986 Kunaev dismissed as leader of Kazakh Communist Party; riots in Alma-Ata
1989 Riots at Novy Uzen; attacks on Caucasians by Kazakhs lead to the evacuation of 5,000 Caucasians; antinuclear

protests by Kazakhs in Moscow and Alma-Ata
1990 Explosion at a nuclear fuel processing plant at Ust-Kamenogorsk causes a leak of toxic gas
1991 Attempted coup in Moscow against Gorbachev; the Soviet Union dissolves; Kazakhstan becomes an independent state within the Commonwealth of Independent States

INDEX

agriculture 4, 7, 8, 15, 18, 21-24, 27, 28
Akayev, Askar 27
Alash Orda 14, 15, 26
Alma-Ata 8, 18, 19
Andropov, Yuri 19
Aral Sea 8, 24
army 25

Baikonur space station 25
Belarus 6, 7, 21, 24
Bolsheviks 14, 15
Brezhnev, Leonid 18, 19

Caspian Sea 8, 24
Caucasians 9
Chernenko, Konstantin 19
China 26
C.I.S. 4, 7, 21
cities 29
Civil War 14, 15
collectivization 7, 15, 17
communism 4, 9, 13-15, 20, 21
corruption 19, 20
Cossacks 12
Crimea 16, 17, 23

democracy 26, 27
deportations 6, 16, 17, 23

ecology 7, 8, 21, 24
ethnic problems 9, 16, 17, 20-23
European Community 26

famine 15
free economic zones 26

Genghis Khan 11

geography 8
glasnost 20
Golden Horde 11
Gorbachev, Mikhail 20, 21

herding 10, 15
hordes 11, 12
horses, Kazakh 10

industry 6, 7, 9, 18, 21, 22, 26-29
Iran 24, 25
irrigation 8
Islam 9, 13, 24
Islamic Renaissance Party 24

Kara Kum 8
Kassim Khan 11
Kazakh people 6-9, 11-12
khanate 11
Khrushchev, Nikita 18, 19, 31
Kirgiz 12
Kolbin, Gennadii 20, 21
Kunaev, Dinmukhamed 18-20, 31
Kyrgyzstan 25, 27

language 21, 29
Lenin, Vladimir 13, 14

Meskhetians 17, 23
Mongols 11, 16

natural resources 4, 6, 27, 28
Nazarbayev, Nursultan 7, 21, 22, 24-26, 31
Nicholas II 13, 14
Nogais 11
nomads 10, 11, 15
nuclear weapons 9, 21, 24, 25

Orda 11
Oyrats 12

Pakistan 26
peoples 8, 9, 22, 23
perestroika (openness) 20, 21
privatization 21, 26
purges 15, 17, 19

religion 29
Russia 4, 6-9, 12, 13, 18, 21, 22, 24-26
Russian Revolution 4, 14, 15

security 24, 25
Semipalatinsk Oblast Peace Committee 21
Siberia 7, 8, 16
Slavs 7, 13, 22, 24
Soviet Germans 16, 17, 22, 23
Soviet Union 4, 6, 7, 9, 14-19
Stalin, Joseph 15-18, 23

Tatars 13, 16, 17, 23
Tauke Khan 12
transportation 29
Tselinograd 23
Turkic 9, 17
Turkish empire 11

Ukraine 6, 7, 9, 12, 18, 21, 22, 24
Uzbekistan 11, 17, 19

Virgin Lands, 18, 22

White Horde 11
World War I 13
World War II 9, 15-17, 23

PHOTOCREDITS

All the pictures in this book were supplied by Novosti R.I.A. apart from page 10 bottom: The Hutchison Library; pages 22, 23, 27 top, 30 left, 31 left & right: Frank Spooner Pictures; page 30 right: Popperfoto.